DAVID L. BERRY, M.D.

CHA-CHING
W(image)SDOM

123 PRACTICAL UNIVERSAL TRUTHS ABOUT MONEY

(A Simple Prescription for Financial Success)

EMERALD
BOOK CO.

Published by Emerald Book Company
Austin, TX
www.emeraldbookcompany.com

Distributed by Emerald Book Company

For ordering information or special discounts for bulk purchases, please contact Emerald Book Company at PO Box 91869, Austin, TX 78709, 512.891.6100.

Design and composition by Greenleaf Book Group LLC
Cover design by Greenleaf Book Group LLC

Publisher's Cataloging-In-Publication Data
(Prepared by The Donohue Group, Inc.)
Berry, David L.
    Cha-ching wisdom : 123 practical universal truths about money : a simple prescription for financial success / David L. Berry.—1st ed.
    p. ; cm.
    ISBN: 978-1-934572-63-4
    1. Finance, Personal—Quotations, maxims, etc. 2. Conduct of life—Quotations, maxims, etc. 3. Finance, Personal—Anecdotes. I. Title.

HG179 .B47 2011
332.024   2010933177

Part of the Tree Neutral® program, which offsets the number of trees consumed in the production and printing of this book by taking proactive steps, such as planting trees in direct proportion to the number of trees used: www.treeneutral.com

Printed in the United States of America on acid-free paper

11 12 13 14 15   10 9 8 7 6 5 4 3 2 1

First Edition

PREFACE

The sound bite has become a staple of American society during the late twentieth and early twenty-first centuries. Our high-tech, fast-paced daily existence has led to many of us developing thirty-second attention spans. PDAs, cell phones, and laptops with Wi-Fi were supposed to make our lives more efficient and more enjoyable so we could spend more time with the ones we love. Unfortunately, this idea has backfired. We are busier and more productive now than ever, but with added stress and less free time. We all want to take a pill for anything that ails us. We want immediate gratification, and we want to spend as little time as possible solving the most complex life circumstances.

We want to take a Prozac, Paxil, or Zoloft to solve thirty years of turmoil and an unfulfilled life. We crave a quick-fix pill to cure smoking, overeating, and anxiety.

In an effort to present some valuable wisdom in this hectic era, I have expanded on the ancient Chinese method of presenting universal truths as proverbs. Each statement on each page of this book may speak volumes to you, or it may strike you as a silly saying that makes you smile based on your own life experience. Either way, I have attempted to keep the message clear and concise, and limited to one or two sentences. Each statement is then explained with examples and anecdotes that add humor or a new perspective to the heavy topics that plague the lives of each of us. My prayer is that this simple book can inspire you (yes, you) to reach further and follow your dreams while simultaneously avoiding common pitfalls in your financial life.

CONTENTS

earn
WISELY

YOUR BEST FRIEND'S IDEA WILL NEVER BE WHAT'S BEST FOR YOUR MONEY.

BRIGHT IDEAS RUN RAMPANT. THIS IS PART OF THE "MILLIONAIRE without working" culture to which nearly every American aspires. Who better to look after you and your hard-earned cash than your old high school drinking buddy? Who wants to say no to a friend, especially someone in whom you have already invested so much of your only real resource—your time?

IN BUSINESS, NEVER BE THE FIRST OR THE LAST IN A PRODUCT PATHWAY. ALWAYS CHOOSE TO BE THE MIDDLEMAN.

THE GUY WHO GROWS THE COTTON GETS FARM SUBSIDIES FROM the US government just to get by eating Ramen noodles. The girl who buys the Egyptian cotton 800-thread-count king-size sheets coughs up $350 for twenty cents' worth of material and overseas child labor. Meanwhile, Ralph Lauren and Pottery Barn make a killing by moving an item from place to place and relabeling it. A middleman may not add any value to a good or service, but he does profit the most from it.

WORKING HARDER IF YOU DO NOT OWN THE BUSINESS IS AN EXERCISE IN FUTILITY.

REMEMBER THE ANTIDRUG PSA FROM THE EIGHTIES WHERE THE GUY says, "I do coke so I can work longer, so I can earn more, so I can do more coke, so I can work longer, so I can earn more . . ." and so on? Such is the American way! Investing more than an eight-hour day can bring you the type of sanity seen in the movie *Fight Club*. As Brad Pitt says in the film, "We are consumers . . . Advertising has us chasing cars and clothes, working jobs that we hate so we can buy sh#@ we don't need." Running on the gerbil wheel for the sake of nothing is the fastest way to suicide—both financially and literally.

CHOOSE TO WORK YOURSELF OUT OF THE JOB OF BEING AN EMPLOYEE.

WORKING FOR SOMEONE ELSE IS A GREAT WAY TO LEARN. BUT MAKE sure you actually learn! Complacency and lack of higher goals are the keys to a miserable existence as "the victim." Use your time as an employee to learn how to play the game. Learn how to attract skilled, loyal employees and learn how to provide an exceptional product or service. Then, do it yourself! Life-satisfaction is usually not congruent with staying in the same job for forty-five years and hoping to God that your employer has planned well for your retirement.

FAIR AND EQUITABLE TRADE BENEFITS EVERYONE; DISHONESTY CHEATS EVERYONE.

WHAT HAPPENS WHEN SOMEONE PROVIDES A GOOD OR SERVICE AND charges ten times the going price just because he can (e.g., price gouging at the hardware store just prior to a hurricane)? The salesman might think his customer a sucker, but guilt and remorse will soon catch him. And what happens to the sucker? He will build resentment and a desire for revenge because he feels taken. That broken storefront window two years later may not have been an accident.

PEOPLE WILL ONLY STEAL FROM YOU OR CHEAT YOU WHEN MONEY, WOMEN, OR WHISKEY IS INVOLVED.

WHAT A GREAT LINE! MY FATHER, THE OMNISCIENT PATRIARCH, COULD always simplify complex human behaviors with such one-liners. One might argue that power is another reason people cheat each other. I would respond that if you can buy a $1,000 bottle of whiskey or champagne for the most beautiful woman in town and drive around with her in a new $100,000 car, wouldn't you feel powerful? And, wouldn't you be the biggest target for fraud or theft?

WHY WOULD ANY BUSINESS PAY $7.25 PER HOUR FOR THE LABOR OF A DISGRUNTLED LOCAL EMPLOYEE WHEN $1 PER HOUR WILL BUY A LOYAL EMPLOYEE OVERSEAS?

MANY AMERICANS MIGHT VILIFY THE SELLING OUT OF AMERICA. But how did America become a great free-enterprise country? Not by an employer hiring uninspired workers who have a labor union harassing the employer to do more for the employees for less work in return. What open-market, publicly traded business would readily pay a higher price for an inferior product (the worker, in this case)? The open market demands that the business get as much as it can for as little money as possible . . . and national pride doesn't satisfy the profit margins.

YOUR MANTRA SHOULD BE "WORK LESS, EARN MORE."

IS SUCH THINKING CONSIDERED GREEDY? WHO CARES! FREE ENTERPRISE is based on greed. Just ask Gordon Gekko, from the movie *Wall Street*. Maybe we should all be looking for a way to work ourselves completely out of working. Six years ago, my personal goal became to work less and earn more. Since that time, my 120-hour workweeks have become 30 hours in the office and 4 to 5 hours at the hospital each week, and I have tripled my salary and increased my investments a hundredfold. Admittedly, I did have to put in those 120-hour workweeks for many, many years, but it has paid off—and will continue to pay off.

THE CONCEPT OF MULTIPLE STREAMS OF INCOME IS THE SAFEST WAY TO ENSURE A RICH AND FULFILLING FUTURE.

ONE JOB FROM 8 A.M. TO 5 P.M., MONDAY THROUGH FRIDAY, MAY seem fulfilling and may be your only perceived responsibility, but you will *always* live from paycheck to paycheck with such a mentality. Receiving royalties from a book, and dividends on investments, and rent from real estate, and income from a patented idea, a day job, and a consulting business on the side constitutes a much better plan.

THE EXPERTS, MEDIA, AND GOVERNMENT REPORTS LIE.

THIS CANNOT BE BREAKING NEWS TO MANY OF YOU. IF CNN REPORTS a minimal rise in the core inflation, pay very close attention. They may also note that oil hit a record high. Core Inflation excludes (by design) energy and food costs. Now, think about it . . . oil goes up 50 percent in twelve months or the US Dollar Index drops by 30 percent, and the prices of goods and services have not changed! Look out! Corporate profits are about to hit the skids because you and I can't afford to drive to the Gap anymore, even for the clearance rack.

THINKING INSIDE THE BOX WILL MAKE YOU A FOLLOWER FOREVER.

THINKING OUTSIDE THE BOX LEADS TO RIDICULE, FOLLOWED BY crucifixion, followed by sainthood. Every truly new idea is deemed crazy (Christopher Columbus) and will lead to near-death experiences, mutiny, or worse. But all great minds will tolerate and endure through the turmoil and emerge as prosperous and wealthy.

SELL YOUR PRODUCT WITH A KEY COMPONENT THAT HAS A LIMITED LIFE SPAN.

FAILURE BY DESIGN MAKES THIS COUNTRY GREAT. EVERYONE KNOWS that we have the technology to have a light bulb work for life. But if you sell enough of these magical "never fail" devices, you will eventually put yourself out of a job. Once everyone owned a reliable computer, the computer companies had to create the concept of upgrades. Since a computer still worked eight years after its purchase, the "new and improved" product had to replace the old one, or the company would ultimately suffer from zero sales. For my word-processing needs, give me the Commodore 64!

AT SOME POINT, THE MARKET WILL ALWAYS BECOME SATURATED.

UNLIMITED WANTS AND LIMITED RESOURCES ARE THE REALITIES OF human existence. Supply and demand economics makes complete sense to most of us. High demand and low supply = high prices. High supply and no demand = a failing business plan. Your market always needs to expand or your product needs to expire and be replaced to continually grow your business.

FOLLOWING THE PATH OF LEAST RESISTANCE IS THE FASTEST ROUTE TO SERFDOM.

THE PAIN-FREE PATH IS LIKELY THE EASIEST, WHICH IS LIKELY TO attract the most people. This country is great because of the uniqueness of its people, not the squished-out premolded citizen that looks and acts and works like everyone else. Work hard. Be unique. Provide a novel product or service, and don't be afraid of the difficult path.

BAKE SOME OF YOUR HALF-BAKED IDEAS. YOU WILL BE AMAZED WHERE THEY TAKE YOU.

MY NINETEEN-YEAR-OLD DAUGHTER ALWAYS GAVE ME TROUBLE about my silly, half-baked ideas. I, of course, took her words as a challenge. My first fully baked idea brought in $90,000, which I used to pay for my dream car. The 2004 Lotus Esprit was an idea twenty-two years in the making (a tenth-grade dream) that finally came true at age thirty-nine. Thanks, Caitlyn!

PREPARING FOR STANDARDIZED TESTING THROUGHOUT YOUR LIFE STANDARDIZES *YOU* TO THE LOWEST COMMON DENOMINATOR.

KNOWLEDGE FOR THE SAKE OF KNOWLEDGE IS USUALLY NOT BENEFICIAL. If everyone is stamped from the same educational mold, it lowers each of our abilities instead of celebrating our differences. Thrive on the unique gifts that *you* bring to the world—and *bring it!*

PASSION AND INDEPENDENT THOUGHT ARE YOUR MOST VALUABLE ASSETS.

GOD GAVE US ALL THE ABILITY TO CONSIDER, THINK, ANALYZE, AND create. A computer can do the calculations in a fixed data set better, faster, and more accurately than you can. So bring into the world that which a computer cannot. Bring in your fire, your love, your enthusiasm, and your soul. Everything else will work itself out.

WHETHER YOU MAKE MINIMUM WAGE OR $500,000 PER YEAR, YOU MAY STILL BE AT THE MERCY OF THE MAN.

THE MAN IS THE EMPLOYER OR THE CORPORATION THAT HOLDS YOUR future in its hands. More broadly, anyone or anything on which your financial success depends can be considered The Man. Why give up your own personal power to someone else? A higher wage doesn't make you immune from victimization. Certainly, learn from the experience of working for The Man while you have to. Let The Man show you how—and how not—to work; if you pay attention, he can be your stepping-stone to independence and completeness.

A "QUICK BUCK" MAY LAND YOU IN JAIL.

EVERY QUICK BUCK OR GREAT IDEA OR WINNING HORSE OR SURE-THING stock or guaranteed business deal should send up red flags in your gut.

"Just hold this for me."

"I'll turn that $100 into $1,000 in a week."

"I'll have the money back in your account before you even miss it."

When someone presents you with a get-rich-quick scheme, run!

INVESTMENT IN EXPANDING YOUR PRACTICAL, USABLE KNOWLEDGE IS THE BEST INVESTMENT YOU WILL EVER MAKE.

EDUCATION IS *ALWAYS* GOOD. EDUCATION IN PRACTICAL, TANGIBLE skills is golden. If you want to learn how to do something, ask someone who has done it—particularly if they have tried a hundred times and failed ninety-nine of them.

INSULATE YOUR INCOME
WITH A NEW IDEA EVERY YEAR.

INCREASE YOUR RISK—AND YOUR WEALTH—WITH NEW VENTURES
each year. You will try and you will fail, but try anyway. Pick new
ventures that seem valid and have manageable worst-case scenarios.
Try a new one at least once each year.

IF YOU BECOME PARALYZED WITH FEAR,
DO SOMETHING ELSE.

MEDICAL MALPRACTICE FEARS DISABLED MANY OF MY FRIENDS WHO were great physicians and healers. Once they began doubting their every decision and every move in surgery, once they could not function because of fear, they lost all of their healing powers. If such a thing happens to you, choose a new path that fills your soul with joy. Choose a path where there is no disabling fear.

WHY PRETEND THAT YOU ARE TOO OLD TO START SOMETHING NEW?

SURE, THERE ARE ALL KINDS OF EXCUSES. SURE, EVERYONE WILL laugh at you. Sure, you will look stupid. Is playing it safe a good way to really live? If it is your dream or aspiration, as Nike says, "Just do it!"

ALWAYS STRIVE TO BE THE EXPERT AT SOMETHING.

BE THE GO-TO PERSON FOR AT LEAST ONE THING. BE THE ONLY ONE who knows how to use the machine that goes "Ping!" Be the only one in town who can bend wood into a circle. Be the only plumber who can fix a leak using an egg and some tongs. Be the only transplant surgeon in town. Have the best fajitas in Austin. Do any little thing. Just be the best at it.

spend
WISELY

A USED CAR SALESMAN IS LYING TO YOU ONLY WHEN HIS LIPS MOVE.

MOST OF US ARE AWARE OF WHEN WE ARE ABOUT TO BE TAKEN—particularly to the cleaners. The problem is that even when we know we are about to be sold a bill of goods, we can't help but to listen and believe in the pipe dream and "buy, Buy, BUY" that which we do not need. Truly wake up and be okay with saying "No!"

THE QUICKEST FIX IS ALSO THE MOST EXPENSIVE.

A GUY DRIVING DOWN THE STREET SEES YOUR CAR, WHICH HAS A FEW old dents. "For $150 I can fix those dents," he says to your spouse. Sounds good, since he works at the body shop you were going to use anyway. Dents come out, but, oh, the spray paint he used didn't quite match. He gives you $50 back and leaves. Everyone makes fun of your two-tone Ford Expedition until you spend the $1,500 on repairing the repair by repainting the whole vehicle.

WHEN IT COMES TO MATTERS OF GOVERNMENT, MEDICAL CARE, AND HOME OR CAR REPAIR, YOU HAVE THREE OPTIONS (BUT YOU MAY PICK ONLY TWO): 1) GOOD, 2) CHEAP, AND 3) FAST.

I WAS AT A CAMPAIGN FUND-RAISER FOR A 2004 US PRESIDENTIAL candidate (Dennis Kucinich, D-Ohio). As a doctor, I felt compelled to ask this brave soul which of the three he was willing to sacrifice in order to assure a stable health-care system. He muttered something about how his plan included the health care of the highest quality that was affordable and readily available to everyone. I just laughed. When the health-care bill passed on March 25, 2010, under the veil of these same three promises, I cried.

IF IT APPRECIATES IN VALUE, BUY IT;
IF IT DEPRECIATES, LEASE IT.

Q: WHAT IS AN ASSET?

A: *Something that appreciates in value.*

Q: WHAT IS A LIABILITY?

A: *Something that depreciates in value.*

LEASING SOMETHING THAT APPRECIATES OVER TIME WILL ALWAYS divorce you from your money. When you spend $900,000 on that office space over seven years and walk away with nothing to show for it— while the building owner used your money to pay his debt on his appreciating building—you will see that lease as his asset and your liability.

MONEY ISN'T EVERYTHING, EXCEPT TO THOSE WHO HAVE NONE.

TELL THE MOTHER WHO CANNOT FEED OR CLOTHE HER CHILDREN that money isn't everything. Given that circumstance, see if you can even utter these words in her presence. My guess is that, unless you are the most callous human being on the planet, you will be incapable of doing it. Only those who have money can possible think such a thought.

THERE IS NO TIME TO FEED YOUR SOUL WHEN YOU CAN'T FEED YOUR STOMACH.

MASLOW'S HIERARCHY OF NEEDS IS INDEED TRUE; BASIC HUMAN needs must be addressed before we can have the luxury of contemplating philosophy or the meaning of life. Once the basics are covered, then you can seek out the job that feeds your soul.

BANKRUPTCY IS THE FASTEST WAY TO A NEW LINE OF CREDIT.

ONE OF MY EMPLOYEES GOT DIVORCED AND FILED FOR BANKRUPTCY to discharge a considerable personal debt. On the day that his debt discharge was finalized by the courts, Citibank issued him a card, already activated with a $100,000 line of credit. Since my friend had just defaulted on about $15,000 to Citibank, he was confused. The call went to their customer service rep, who notified my employee that he was a great credit risk because he could not declare bankruptcy again for ten more years.

WHEN YOU TAKE A CASH ADVANCE FROM PAYDAY LOANS OR YOUR CREDIT CARD, YOU ARE IN SERIOUS TROUBLE.

CASH ADVANCES ARE GREAT IF YOU ARE BUYING AN APPRECIATING asset with a zero-interest signature loan. Unfortunately, this is never the case with your Visa card. Eighteen to 25 percent interest is the rule on cash advances, and there is usually a fee for this service. Payday loans may exceed 100 percent interest. Flexibility is what you are being offered, but this type of flexibility may be the last stake in the coffin of your financial death.

LOTTERY TICKET SALES GO UP WHEN THE ECONOMY GOES DOWN.

MORE POVERTY BEGETS MORE DESPERATION, WHICH BEGETS MORE panic. The true regressive tax is the lottery ticket. The majority of tickets are sold to the poor and destitute, who are hoping and praying in vain for that miracle that will somehow save them from poverty. Don't be a putz; take that dollar and buy a loaf of bread or a new razor to use before your next job interview.

IT IS FAR BETTER TO SPEND MONEY ON PROZAC THAN TO SPEND MONEY ON OBSESSIVE SHOPPING.

I AM CONVINCED THAT ANY OBSESSIVE OR ADDICTIVE BEHAVIOR IS THE result of failing to follow the soul's true path. Although I do not recommend medicating your pain away, sometimes medical intervention can halt the vicious cycle of addictive behavior. If you find yourself in the trap of addiction, seek medication as an adjunctive aid, but not as the solution. Then, search your soul and your resources for a permanent solution. By doing so, you will find your sole (soul) purpose.

IF YOU DON'T USE IT FOR THIRTY DAYS, GET RID OF IT.

IS LIFE REALLY ABOUT WHO CAN ACCUMULATE THE MOST CRAP IN their house before they die? (See *Hoarding: Buried Alive* on The Learning Channel.) If items in your life do not serve the creation of who you truly are, they are weighing you down. Get rid of them. Clutter serves no purpose except to cover up the true meaning of your reality and of your life.

IF YOU ARE BUYING SOMETHING TO IMPRESS YOUR NEIGHBOR, DON'T.

IT WON'T IMPRESS HIM ANYWAY. HE MIGHT JUDGE YOU OR THINK of you as a jerk because you buy that fancy new car or riding lawn mower or power tool. She might comment on that pretty skirt or dress or necklace while "dissing" you to your mutual friends. You are now responsible for your neighbor coveting your ass (especially if you buy the fat donkey).

ONLY SPEND MONEY ON HOME IMPROVEMENT IF IT RAISES THE VALUE OF YOUR HOME MORE THAN THE AMOUNT YOU ARE SPENDING.

HOME IMPROVEMENTS ARE ALWAYS A GOOD IDEA, BUT DON'T GET carried away. Basic maintenance is essential. The drawbridge across your pond may not be. Be honest and calculate whether this improvement maintains your value or increases your value. When in doubt, ask a real estate agent for their input.

A LOTTERY WINNER WILL NEVER MANAGE HIS ASSETS WELL.

HOW MANY STORIES HAVE YOU HEARD ABOUT THE LONG-TERM outcome of an instant millionaire's good fortune? I'd be willing to bet a valued body part that things didn't end up well. When faced with megabucks, the new winner probably either went crazy buying stuff he thought he always deserved, or he realized that money didn't buy happiness, which resulted in despair and more misery than before.

A DOLLAR, IN AND OF ITSELF, HAS ABSOLUTELY NO VALUE.

THE ART, INK, AND PAPER OF A DOLLAR BILL DO HAVE SOME VALUE. (Although, unfortunately, the art has been copied so many times that it has lost much of its value.) In times past, the dollar could be redeemed for silver or was backed by national gold reserves in Fort Knox (assuming there was any gold left). Not anymore. A dollar is what is commonly referred to as "fiat currency"—worth absolutely nothing except by mutual agreement and delusion.

ATTORNEYS ARE THE ONLY ONES WHO WIN IN ANY LAWSUIT—EVER.

THERE ARE GOOD FIGHTS, AND THERE ARE THOSE WHO PROFIT FROM a good fight. If you choose to die fighting in a ditch, remember: it is you and the other guy dying while the lawyers are laughing all the way to the bank (with your money).

A GOOD CONTRACT IS WORTH ITS WEIGHT IN SILVER.

AN OUNCE OF SILVER IS WORTH ABOUT THE SAME VALUE AS THE high-quality linen paper that your contract is printed on, which probably cost you about $800 in legal fees to draw up. If one of the parties to this agreement is put out, he or she will break the contract. So, don't get hung up in the contract, get hung up in the face-to-face agreement that led to the contract.

A GOOD HANDSHAKE IS WORTH ITS WEIGHT IN PLUTONIUM.

SEE THE PREVIOUS PAGE FOR FURTHER EXPLANATION.

A COLLEGE DEGREE WAS WORTH SOMETHING
WHEN NOT EVERYONE HAD ONE.

DON'T GET ME WRONG: I AM A BIG BELIEVER IN COLLEGE EDUCATION. I have one problem, though. Once you get an MBA and fifty thousand other grads with MBAs are looking for the very job to which you are applying, don't be surprised if your MBA gets you work flipping burgers for minimum wage. Following the crowd will get you the same job and the same paycheck as the crowd . . . if you are lucky.

ALWAYS BUY A USED, DEALER-CERTIFIED CAR WITH A SHORT-TERM WARRANTY.

NEW CARS DEPRECIATE IMMEDIATELY. WOULD YOU VOLUNTARILY throw $10,000 out the window as you drive off the parking lot? That is exactly what happens when you get skinned for a new car so your ego can go for a ride. Go with the used car that looks good and comes with a one-year warranty. Any lemon will go bad within a year.

BUYING AN EXTENDED WARRANTY IS GIVING YOUR MONEY TO A BUSINESS TWICE—YOU ARE BETTING THAT THE COMPANY HAS AN INFERIOR PRODUCT.

IF YOU BOUGHT A LEMON, YOU WIN! STICK WITH SHORT-TERM warranties and buy them only on used products. Check *Consumer Reports* to avoid the lemons altogether.

FINANCIAL INDEPENDENCE MEANS BECOMING SELF-SUSTAINING, WITHOUT THE NEED TO WORK AGAIN, EVER.

EVERYONE HAS AN IDEA OF WHAT IT MEANS TO BE RICH, BUT BEING rich is only an idea. Financial independence, though, is a tangible, achievable process that involves income and outgo. When the income is greater than the outgo, without you having to work day-to-day and paycheck-to-paycheck, you win!

THE BIGGER THE VISIBLE ASSETS, THE BIGGER THE TARGET.

WHEN ONE FLAUNTS ABUNDANCE, ONE BECOMES A LIKELY TARGET for those who wish for abundance. Living simply (millionaire-next-door style) causes little commotion. Blending in might be the best way to avoid both burglary and IRS tax-evasion investigations.

QUALITY IS WORTH THE EXTRA COST.

IF YOU ARE LOOKING FOR DISPOSABLE STUFF, GO TO OLD NAVY OR Target or Walmart. If you want to keep your shoes for ten years, buy Johnston & Murphy or Cole Haan. Kids grow out of their stuff too quickly to buy highest quality, so send them to Walmart. But once your feet stop growing, buy at a higher price and keep the shoes.

CAR AND HOME MAINTENANCE IS ALWAYS WORTH THE EXPENSE.

LETTING YOUR BIGGEST INVESTMENTS DETERIORATE IS A BAD IDEA. An ounce of prevention really is worth a pound of cure. Let the garbage rot. Don't let your $350,000 house rot.

NEVER SELL AN ITEM OF SENTIMENTAL VALUE FOR ANY AMOUNT OF CASH.

I HEARD A STORY ABOUT A TWENTY-YEAR-OLD HOPELESS ROMANTIC who spent $7,900 on a gorgeous engagement ring. It had a beautiful 1.15-karat diamond marquis center stone and the highest quality baguettes on each side. He spent his life's savings on the love of his life. Ten years later, the young couple was strapped for cash, so, in a time of desperation, she hocked the ring for $3,500 without telling her husband. The money paid off some old debt and was gone in a few weeks—but the ring was gone forever. Never do such a thing. Sacrifice dinners out or a summer vacation. Don't sacrifice a memory.

DIGGING IN THE COUCH TO FIND PENNIES TO BUY BREAD MAKES YOU APPRECIATE PENNIES.

IT SUCKS TO BE POOR. RUNNING UP TO TEXACO TO BUT BREAD AND diapers on the 22-percent credit card is insane, but sometimes it is the only option. When your life depends on simple things, you learn to appreciate them like never before. During my OB/GYN residency I supported two kids and a wife on a 100-hour-per-week job that paid $18,350 per year. It was not a recipe for financial abundance. Remember the hard times and have empathy for those going through them.

IT'S ALL ABOUT ADDITION AND SUBTRACTION— MAINLY SUBTRACTION.

THERE IS NEVER A DEPOSIT THAT I FORGET TO RECORD, BUT THERE IS always a debit or check that I forget to record. Income and salaries are predictable. Why not make expenses as predictable as possible? Subtraction surprises are never good surprises.

DO I REALLY HAVE MONEY IN MY CHECKBOOK IF I HAVE CHECKS LEFT?

SPENDING THE SAME MONEY TWICE JUST BECAUSE CHECKS ARE IN the checkbook or a credit card is in your wallet leads to pain and anguish. Although it seems silly to think this way, we're not talking about the logical center of your brain. The emotional center says, "I need that new widget to make me feel strong and powerful and complete and happy." It's like *The Missing Piece* by Shel Silverstein. Acknowledge and feed the emotional part of your brain. Just do it as inexpensively as you can.

PAY YOURSELF FIRST.

IF YOU PAY ALL THE BILLS AND BUY ALL THE GROCERIES AND THE kids' clothes and tutoring for little Johnny's math and the new car sound system and the fabulous birthday party and then put what's left over into savings, you will have no savings. There is no such thing as extra money. Pay yourself first, then pay the bills. You will find a way to survive without the extraneous expenses and you will have an intact savings account.

MORE MONEY WON'T FIX MORE DEBT.

TAKE SOMEONE WHO HAS $10,000 IN CREDIT CARD DEBT THAT HE is slowly paying off. Now, double his salary. I will bet you that the first thing that happens is his credit card debt triples. Without a fundamental change in your relationship with money, you will continue down the pathway you have been on, even if you acquire more money. It's just like Sir Isaac Newton's first law of motion, which says that an object in motion will remain in motion and an object at rest will remain at rest unless either is acted upon by an outside force. For you, that outside force must be your conscious and purposeful rewiring of your financial brain and your actions.

LEAVE YOUR EMOTIONS AT THE DOOR WHEN BUYING ANYTHING.

EMOTIONAL PURCHASES WILL LEAVE YOU FEELING EMPTY AND broke. If you want to buy something to make yourself feel important or powerful, buy a monthly membership to Doctors Without Borders or Save the Children Foundation or some other worthy charitable cause. That way, you can feel important and powerful and help someone at the same time. (A tax deduction is the bonus prize at the year's end!)

GO FOR THE GENERIC BRAND OF PRESCRIPTION DRUGS.

THERE ARE STRINGENT CRITERIA FOR GENERIC DRUGS. THEY MAY not be the Scotch tape of the industry, but they do the same job for one-eighth the price. If you insist on a brand name, make it a brand-name dishwasher or some other durable household device.

DRUG COMPANIES PRICE DRUGS TO REIMBURSE THEMSELVES FOR YEARS OF RESEARCH AND DEVELOPMENT IN LESS THAN TWELVE MONTHS OF SALES.

THEREFORE, THE PRICE OF THE DRUG STILL UNDER PATENT IS EIGHT to ten times the actual worth of that product. Just look at Zantac or Pepcid now that they are over-the-counter drugs. They used to be a buck a pill; now, ten bucks will buy you forty.

ALL BLEEDING STOPS—EVENTUALLY.

NOT TO BE MORBID, BUT IN MEDICAL SCHOOL, THIS TRUISM pertained to the decision between cure and death. It can also apply to financial hemorrhaging; the financial bleeding will definitely stop at some point. You may either deal with the cause of the hemorrhage or die a financial death by ignoring it. The choice is yours.

A "GOLD" OR "PLATINUM" ANYTHING IS MADE OF NEITHER GOLD NOR PLATINUM.

THE GOLD CARD AND THE PLATINUM MEMBERSHIP ARE CLEVER WAYS of divorcing you from your money. Do you really think you are an "important" person because you have the best of the best and board the same plane as the rest of the hotshots on the red carpet? Ego, ego, ego! Someone is playing you like a fiddle. Don't bother with the color of your credit card. Bother with no annual fees and low APRs. I'll take the Talc or the Zinc Card if the terms are right.

WHY DO WE STRIVE TO IMPRESS STRANGERS WHOM WE CARE NOTHING ABOUT?

THE DEALER AT THE BLACKJACK TABLE NEEDS TO KNOW THAT I'M A high roller, so I have to have my $500 sunglasses (and bet at the $5 table). The tennis mom has to have the boob job to impress the country club snobs whom she hates and the cute lifeguard who won't give her the time of day. What are we *doing*?

LITTLE DAILY SPENDING HABITS ADD UP QUICKLY.

THE $2 TO $5 SPENT DAILY ON SNACKS OR COFFEE ADDS UP TO between $730 and $1,825 per year. Multiply that by ten years at 10 percent interest and you have well over ten grand in coffee. Thirsty still?

THE MINIMUM PAYMENT PROGRAM WILL KEEP YOU IN DEBT TO THE CREDIT CARD COMPANY FOR THIRTY-FIVE YEARS.

TAKE THE COFFEE MONEY AND PUT IT TOWARD YOUR CREDIT CARD debt. For $10,000 and thirty-five years of your life, you can make your own coffee.

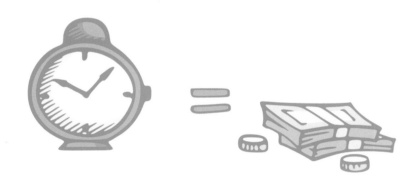

plan
WISELY

THE VALUE OF MONEY OVER TIME IS COMPLETELY IGNORED IN OUR SOCIETY: START SAVING EARLY.

WHAT WOULD HAPPEN IF YOUR SIXTEEN-YEAR-OLD WORKED OVER the summer, put $3,000 into a Roth IRA, and forgot about it until retirement? About $500,000 would be in the kitty at that time. Why is it that we all wait until later to save? Even $1 per day when we start our first job would lead to a massive accumulation of wealth.

WHEN OIL IS UP, THE STOCK MARKET IS DOWN.

WAY DOWN, USUALLY. MOST OF US HAVE FORGOTTEN THE LESSONS OF the past. What is stagflation again? In this day and age, oil prices are tied to absolutely every aspect of every good and service that can be imagined. Unless you are a self-sufficient, self-sustaining organic farmer who needs to buy nothing and sell nothing, you are affected by the price of oil. High oil prices are inflationary, which takes your money out of the marketplace. Less money to invest means you have to sell in order to eat. When everyone has a great investment idea but Warren Buffett is invested only in oil stocks, silver, and Swiss government bonds, go with Warren.

BANKS WILL ONLY LOAN MONEY TO THOSE WHO DO NOT NEED IT.

NEVER A TRUER PHRASE HAS BEEN SPOKEN (OR WRITTEN). THE GUY with $250,000 in savings with Chase or Wells Fargo who wants a $25,000 loan can get a pretty good interest rate. Banks have no problem lending you money that belongs to you in the first place, and they profit besides. But what happens when you hit a bad time with your sleazy general contractor while remodeling that dream home of yours? It takes eighteen months instead of twelve and you and your family can't afford the student loans and the monthly expenses and the kids' schools and the furnished three-bedroom apartment and the original home loan and the construction loan and the storage costs for all of your furniture. Try to get a signature line of credit now, bucko.

DOCUMENT AND ITEMIZE ALL OF YOUR GIFTS TO GOODWILL.

I KNOW. DEDUCTIONS FOR CHARITABLE CONTRIBUTIONS ARE NOT what they used to be, but it makes sense to acknowledge that you are contributing to the good of another human being anyway. If you can take the tax deduction, so be it. If not, at least experience to the highest level the satisfaction of sharing a gift with your fellow man.

THE MOST EXPENSIVE LINE ITEM IN YOUR BUDGET WILL ALWAYS BE TAXES.

DON'T BE FOOLED: UNCLE SAM IS ALWAYS YOUR BIGGEST EXPENSE. The obvious taxes come directly from the paycheck. The ones we complain about are the federal income taxes and some state taxes. But don't forget about sales tax, the death tax (or estate tax), gasoline taxes, the dreaded property tax, Social Security and Medicare taxes, and the potential carbon tax and/or value-added tax being considered now. Capital gains taxes even apply taxes to our post-tax dollars, and they went up with Obamacare. Taxes affect the prices of hotels and rental cars and airline travel and licenses and operations for all sorts of businesses. Well over 50 percent of everyone's gross income goes to taxes.

DOLLAR COST AVERAGING IS A REALLY GOOD IDEA.

THERE IS NO COMMON SENSE IN THE IDEA OF BUYING HIGH AND then continuing to buy low—until you look at a chart. If you buy $100 of gold per month regardless of the price, you will always come out ahead. Even if the price goes up and down and ultimately returns to the same price it was when you began, you will have accumulated a large cache of cash (or gold) for a lower than average price.

IN THE REAL WORLD, THE AMOUNT OF MONEY YOUR INVESTMENT MAKES YOU IN ONE YEAR WILL RARELY EXCEED THE PRINCIPAL AMOUNT INVESTED.

DON'T BE FOOLED BY TRYING TO OUTPERFORM THE GREATEST MUTUAL fund from last year. You will always make a little or lose a little. The key is not what you make off your investments each year. The key is to put away progressively more principal each year. Your greatest asset is your continued productivity.

"BUY AND HOLD" DOESN'T WORK DURING STAGFLATION.

EVERYONE HAS FORGOTTEN WHAT HAPPENS WHEN A TIME OF POOR economic growth occurs concurrently with elevations of consumer prices. The price of oil goes up, the price of everything else goes up, the wages don't go up proportionally, 10 percent inflation hits, everyone has to sell their stocks to buy the GI Joe with the kung-fu grip for their kids at Christmas, stocks go down, and everyone loses. Weathering the storm is fine—for those who can afford such a luxury.

RECESSION BEGINS MONTHS BEFORE ANYONE EVER SPEAKS OF IT.

WE HAVE TO BE IN A RECESSION FOR THREE TO SIX MONTHS BEFORE the "leading economic indicators" for the quarter pick up the message. You will hear of "long-overdue corrections" prior to a disaster.

HISTORY ALWAYS REPEATS ITSELF, USUALLY EVERY THIRTY YEARS.

WE MUST HAVE A WAR EVERY GENERATION SO THAT THE NEWBIES CAN experience its horror and realize that the glory of fighting is fleeting and painful. Such is the case with economic trends also. When we don't learn lessons from the past (such as when we forget about gas-guzzling cars and long lines at the pump), God turns up the volume—and the price—the next time.

HE WHO HAS THE GOLD DOES INDEED MAKE THE RULES.

WHO DOES MAKE RULES? DO ANY OF THE FOLLOWING COME TO MIND? International bankers, the IMF, the county tax assessor, China, big pharmaceutical companies, European central banks, the Vanderbilts, the Morgans, the Rockefellers, the Rothschilds, the Saudi royal family? Many of the biggest global decisions are not made by people or governments but by institutions or underground financial oligarchies. Your real boss is the bank that holds your mortgage. Your real boss is the employer that holds your "secure" retirement. Your real boss is Senator Bill Frist telling your doctors to replace your feeding tube. Power = Money = Control.

COMMODITIES AND REAL ESTATE WILL NEVER BE WORTH ZERO.

MANHATTAN WAS PURCHASED FOR BEADS A FEW HUNDRED YEARS ago. Now, we would agree that the price of the island has increased dramatically. An ounce of gold will always be worth something. A barrel of oil will always be useful, as long as there are gas-powered machines. Prices may fluctuate, but corporate dissolution and bankruptcy are not concerns when it comes to such commodities. Circuit City or GM stock, on the other hand, can go to zero . . . They are only pieces of paper.

INTEREST RATES WILL NEVER GO BELOW ZERO.

EXCEPT IN THE UNLIKELY CIRCUMSTANCE THAT THE BANKS PAY you to take their money, there is no such thing as negative interest. When rates for mortgages were at 20 percent, the fear was of further rate hikes. When thirty-year fixed-rate mortgages went to 5 percent, refinancing should have been mandatory for all nondead humans.

RAW MATERIALS ARE WORTH ALMOST NOTHING. HIGH-TECH MANUFACTURED GOODS ARE WORTH EVERYTHING.

LOOK AT AMERICAN HISTORY. THE AGRARIAN SOUTH AND THE industrial North battled the Civil War over economics. The low profit margin for tobacco and cotton farming required a low-wage or no-wage workforce (slavery), while the North relied on industrial development. Now, manufacturers of simple textiles need sweatshops and illegal workers or NAFTA or overseas plants to turn a profit (Levi's are no longer made in the USA). That is the key to the US exporting our jobs to Southeast Asia or India, and the key to our trade deficit. We export raw goods for minimal profit, reimport the high-end products, and sell them for hundreds of times more than the production cost—and we continue to rack up massive trade deficits every quarter.

YOU WILL NEVER SELL YOUR HOUSE AT THE PRICE YOU WANT AND AT THE TIME YOU NEED.

IT SEEMS OBVIOUS THAT IT'S EXTREMELY UNLIKELY THAT YOU WILL sell your home for what you want, when you want, but no one really understands this concept until they need to sell. Whether you're being relocated by your job, grandma got sick and needs cash, or a divorce hits you between the eyes and the lawyers want a $40,000 retainer, you'll never sell the house for the amount you need. By the way, the same holds true for the buyer!

YOUR HOUSE MAY NOT BE YOUR BEST INVESTMENT.

THERE IS NO YARD WORK REQUIRED FOR A SERIES EE SAVINGS BOND. Your Dell stock certificate isn't taxed every year that you own it (from both the bank and the government). There is no need to repaint your Fidelity Select fund every few years. That 100-ounce bar of silver doesn't spring a leak every two years in the heavy springtime thunderstorms. Obviously, there is simplicity in non-home investments, and you may be paying a hefty price for the luxury of staying in your home. Besides, getting upside down on your mortgage may cause you to reevaluate the morality of "jingle mail"—the phenomenon of a homeowner relinquishing the home to a lender by simply dropping the keys in the mail and walking away.

ADVANCED PLANNING FENDS OFF EVIL SPIRITS.

BAD STUFF IN THE PRACTICE OF MEDICINE ONLY HAPPENS WHEN problems are compounded. The same is true of financial disasters. Oops! No will. Ooops! No revision to my will with the divorce. Oooops! I died. It is almost as if creating a will will keep you alive, just as cross-matching and holding two pints of blood for a patient prior to a simple surgery will seemingly prevent bleeding.

ONE HUNDRED BASE HITS ARE FAR SUPERIOR TO TEN HOME RUNS.

DO THE MATH! EACH BASE HIT IS ONE-FOURTH OF A HOME RUN. ONE hundred times one-fourth is twenty-five runs; compare that with the ten home runs. Or ask any New York cabbie: the tips on ten short fares are considerably better than the tip on one long fare. Strive to have consistency in your financial portfolio and get those base hits time after time. It's boring but it's profitable.

AS TYLER DURDEN SAYS IN *FIGHT CLUB*,
"ON A LONG ENOUGH TIMELINE, THE SURVIVAL RATE
FOR EVERYONE DROPS TO ZERO."

DEATH IS INEVITABLE. PLAN FOR IT.

BUY TERM LIFE INSURANCE
UNTIL YOU CAN SELF-INSURE.

WHY WOULD YOU BUY A LIFE INSURANCE POLICY THAT GIVES YOU limited and poor investment options with a huge commission for the sales guy? Why not buy temporary life insurance, and then, once you don't need a big cash payoff (when the children are grown and house is paid and nest egg is intact), get rid of it?

WHEN IT COMES TO LIFE INSURANCE,
YOU WIN ONLY IF YOU DIE EARLY.

SAY YOU PUT IN $216 PER QUARTER FOR A $500,000 TERM LIFE POLICY. You die after ten years and $8,640 in premiums. Uncle Sam could historically get $250,000 of the total, and your heirs would get around $241,360 in cash. So, actually, they win. The bonus in 2010 was no estate taxes. Your heirs can win big if you plan correctly, but you are still dead.

ESTATE PLANNING IS ONLY USEFUL FOR REDUCING TAXES AFTER YOU ARE DEAD.

GOOD PLANNING IS A GIFT TO THOSE WHO SURVIVE YOU. ESTATE planning is nothing more than simplifying your survivors' tax burden after death. Don't get too hung up on it.

MAKE IT EASY FOR YOUR FAMILY IF YOU WERE TO DIE.

WHEN YOU ARE GONE, IT WON'T BE ABOUT YOU ANYMORE. SO PLAN ahead. Have a will. Have a living will. Don't let the courts decide what happens to your kids or your money. Have a durable power of attorney for health care and finances. Have life insurance that will pay for your funeral and sustain your family.

LETTING A STRANGER DECIDE YOUR CHILDREN'S FATE IN A DIVORCE IS STUPID.

BE CIVIL TO EACH OTHER DURING A DIVORCE, IF ONLY FOR THE SAKE of retaining control over what happens to your children.

WHY WOULD ANY WOMAN
BETWEEN THE AGES OF FIFTEEN AND FIFTY
WITH AN INTACT UTERUS EVER HAVE
HEALTH INSURANCE THAT EXCLUDED PREGNANCY?

ABSURD, AIN'T IT? IT'S LIKE SAYING, "I WANT HEALTH INSURANCE that does not cover accidents or appendicitis." All that happens between ages fifteen and fifty (barring the rare or catastrophic illness) is accidents, appendicitis, and pregnancy.

CHECK YOUR STOCKS AND MUTUAL FUNDS DAILY.
AFTER ALL, IT'S YOUR MONEY.

DON'T DAY TRADE AND PANIC OVER THE DOWNSIDES; MAKE REASONABLE and sober choices. If the oil sector looks good, shift a little more into oil. If the US economy looks terrible, shift a bit more into developing and foreign markets.

B-SHARES ARE FOR MORONS.

B-SHARES ARE SHARES OF STOCK SOLD BY FINANCIAL ADVISORS WHO are looking out for themselves. B-shares allow the salesperson to be paid first, and the salesperson continues to be paid out of all of those hidden fees that no one tells you about. If your advisor starts discussing B-shares, fire him.

PRIVATE PROPERTY IS NEVER FULLY OWNED BY ANYONE IN THE UNITED STATES.

WHAT EVER HAPPENED TO THE IDEA OF SOVEREIGNTY, AND PROPERTY fully owned and controlled by the individual? Property taxes have ballooned to the point that I would owe at least $1,500 per month in property taxes for the rest of my life if I were to live in a nice four-bedroom home in central Austin. Is this real ownership of property?

HOW MUCH OF YOUR PAYCHECK GOES TO FUND LARGE CENTRAL BANKS?

THINK ABOUT IT. TAXES GO TO PAY NATIONAL DEBT, WHICH IS largely owned by foreign interests, including large European central banks, China, and Russia. What about your biggest debt service, your mortgage? Who owns it? JP Morgan Chase? Wells Fargo? Bank of America? How about your car loan? Most likely, very little of this cash gets recirculated in the good ol' US of A.

PLAN FOR YOUR BUSINESS PARTNERSHIPS TO END BADLY.

EVERYONE HOPES FOR GAZILLIONS OF DOLLARS FROM THEIR BUSINESS venture. But the fact is that most businesses fail. Things may go badly, so plan the exit strategy and discuss it with your partners. Sufficient preparation can keep the lawyers from getting rich over your failure.

THE STOCK MARKET IS A SOCIALLY ACCEPTABLE FORM OF GAMBLING, ESPECIALLY IN THE SHORT TERM.

DAY TRADERS ARE SIMPLY GAMBLERS. YOU MIGHT AS WELL GO TO THE casino and enjoy the scenery while you lose your shirt. Even Warren Buffett cannot reliably predict the market. Unless you have inside knowledge (which is illegal), don't bother with short-term trading unless it's purely for the rush of gambling and you can afford to lose. Take the money and go to Vegas instead. Enjoy a show. Spend the cash there.

RECHECK EVERYONE ELSE'S MATH.

IT'S NOT A TRUST ISSUE. TRUST, BUT VERIFY! DON'T DO ALL THE calculations over again; just spot-check it to make sure the accountant isn't cheating you. Pure faith and pure trust are open invitations to be violated. The louder they yell that you don't trust them, the less you should trust them.

FUTURES CONTRACTS AND MARGIN INVESTING ARE REALLY BAD IDEAS.

THESE TWO ARE EXPONENTIALLY MORE RISKY THAN DAY TRADING. It's losing money that you don't have. If you have never seen *Trading Places* with Dan Aykroyd and Eddie Murphy, rent it today. Margin calls suck! Randolph and Mortimer Duke found out in the movie how badly playing with money you don't have can decimate your financial life.

CASH IS INDEED KING,
EXCEPT DURING RUNAWAY INFLATION.

THE ALWAYS-ALMIGHTY DOLLAR HAS NEVER FAILED US. THAT MEANS it will soon. When a dollar is more valuable as fuel for a fire to keep you warm (or as toilet paper), it is not worth much. Look at Germany in the 1920s. Look at Argentina in the late twentieth century. Every society thinks it won't happen to them, but when runaway inflation starts, buy commodities, durable items of sustained value, or tools of a trade.

NEVER UNDERESTIMATE SECURITY, UNLESS IT IS SOCIAL SECURITY.

A SECURE FUTURE BOLSTERED WITH LIFE INSURANCE, ASSURED income for retirement, or a fulfilling career is key to avoiding slavery to our work and a miserable life. Security does not come from the government-sponsored welfare program currently entitled, "the US Social Security system." Do you think that the federal government, the institution that spends two trillion dollars more than it earns each year, is a worthy steward of your money—of your financial future? Plan on Social Security giving you *nothing.*

DO YOU REALLY WANT TO RELY ON THE FEDERAL GOVERNMENT OR YOUR COMPANY FOR A SECURE RETIREMENT?

DO YOU WANT TO SPEND YOUR GOLDEN YEARS ON WELFARE, AS PART of an entitlement program managed by these bureauc(rats)? What guarantee do you have that the government or your employer will not change the rules or go out of business just when you need them the most? A friend of mine who worked for a solo-practice consultant since 1978 learned this the hard way. She chose not to put away money for retirement and refused to sign up for IRAs. She is now sick and entering forced retirement, and she asked the boss about the "retirement plan." Rely on yourself, and plan your own assurances. Don't rely on the assurances of colleagues or strangers.

A MONKEY THROWING DARTS AT *THE WALL STREET JOURNAL* IS MORE SUCCESSFUL THAN THE MOST STUDIED INVESTMENT ADVISORS.

CHOOSING THE BEST INVESTMENT FOR LAST YEAR IS EASY. CHOOSING the best investment for this year is a crapshoot. Stay with the basics of diversity, low costs, no loads, low risk, and stable, well-managed companies.

YOU DON'T HAVE TO PAY A BANK
TO GIVE YOURSELF AN EIGHT-YEAR DISCOUNT
ON YOUR THIRTY-YEAR MORTGAGE.

ALL BANKS AND SOME WISE BOOKS DISCUSS THE BENEFIT OF THE biweekly mortgage payment plan. The idea is to pay half of your monthly mortgage payment every two weeks so that you will pay off the mortgage seven to eight years early. My question is, why would you pay some bank to set up a thirteen-payment-per-year mortgage? You see, every two weeks is twenty-six payments in a fifty-two-week year, which is one extra monthly payment per year. You can do the same by adding 8 to 10 percent to each monthly payment or by making one extra payment per year, preferably as early in the year as possible.

live
WISELY

IS IT OK TO BE JUST OK FOR THE REST OF YOUR LIFE?

WHY IS IT THAT I SEE KIDS AND ADULTS JUST FUNCTIONING, JUST surviving, walking around like the automatons of science fiction? Is your life's purpose to be "just OK" forever? Why would anyone settle for being OK?

BEFORE YOU WERE BORN, DID YOU STAND BEFORE GOD AND CHOOSE TO HAVE AN AVERAGE INCOME, A MEDIOCRE JOB, AND "FAIR TO MIDDLIN'" RELATIONSHIPS?

THERE WOULDN'T BE MANY BOOK SALES IF THE TRASHY NOVELIST wrote of regular people in average circumstances and unremarkable relationships. Is that what we were born to achieve? I want a hot and steamy relationship with the love of my life. I choose to always be in the top 1 percent of wage earners in an exciting job that I can brag about. I am living life and choose not to be the victim of some imagined idea that keeps me down from now until the day I die.

WHAT IF ATTITUDE WERE EVERYTHING?

YOUR MOM USED TO SAY, "WORK HARD AND STAY FOCUSED AND everything will work out fine." The power of positive thinking and all that nonsense—maybe it does really work, and work magically. Try it and find out!

EVERY DAY, YOU SHOULD STRIVE TO LIVE THE WORDS OF GENE KRANZ, FLIGHT DIRECTOR DURING THE *APOLLO 13* PROGRAM: "FAILURE IS NOT AN OPTION!"

WHEN ONE HAS THE MINDSET THAT CERTAIN THINGS ARE COMPLETELY out of the realm of possibility, they usually stay that way. But a "never say die" attitude in the face of seeming impossibility is at the core of the survival of wartime prisoner camps, hostage crises, and Nazi concentration camps. The noblest man in the world is the one who stares failure in the face and wins against all odds. The fact that success is "10 percent inspiration and 90 percent perspiration" is never truer than in the unyielding, focused intention that makes everything that you can imagine well within your reach.

JOSEPH CAMPBELL SAID IT BEST: "FOLLOW YOUR BLISS."

WHERE DOES SERENITY LIE? WHAT REALLY LIGHTS YOUR FIRE? WHAT gives you the feeling of being whole and complete and fully in the moment? Figure out, and do that! The money will come to you in time.

WHAT IS THE GRANDEST VERSION OF THE GREATEST VISION YOU EVER HELD FOR YOURSELF?

AT A SPIRITUAL RETREAT IN ESTES PARK, COLORADO, IN DECEMBER of 1996, I first really understood what Neale Donald Walsch meant by this question. What is the highest, most important, most worthy, most fulfilling idea that you ever thought about who you are? Forget the rules and boundaries we have all made up. Who would you be if you couldn't fail? Be that person!

WHAT IS THE NEXT GRANDEST VERSION OF THE GREATEST VISION YOU EVER HELD FOR YOURSELF?

ONCE YOU HAVE ACHIEVED YOUR GREATEST VISION, WHAT NEXT? WHY not expand your vision and your dreams to the next level? Why should any of us, with our unlimited creativity, ever rest on our laurels?

IF YOU'RE GOING TO PURSUE REVENGE, YOU'D BETTER DIG TWO GRAVES.

WAYNE DYER SPOKE OF THIS ANCIENT CHINESE PROVERB. IT IS INDEED true. If you get into an argument with your business partner because he has wronged you, you want blood. Don't worry. You will have your revenge, and it may be the death of you as well. Unexpressed hatred and anger and chronic urges for revenge cause disease and financial ruin. Just look around. You will see this is true.

ONCE YOU CHOOSE TO BE CONTENT WITH ALL THAT YOU HAVE, DIE.

LIFE IS NOT A GAME TO BE WON. IT IS A CONSTANT CHALLENGE TO reinvent yourself and create new goals and new purposes. You could be eight or eighty and this rule would still hold true. If you completely give up on everything, you will die, usually within a few months.

WHAT YOU GIVE AWAY FREELY REALLY DOES COME BACK TO YOU AT LEAST SEVENFOLD.

SEND WORD TO THE UNIVERSE THAT THERE IS PLENTY. IN FACT, THERE is so much abundance, you are freely giving it away. What better way to experience abundance than to be the source?

SUZE ORMAN IS RIGHT: "PEOPLE FIRST, THEN MONEY, THEN THINGS."

STUFF DOESN'T MAKE YOU HAPPY. GEORGE CARLIN HAS A BIT ON "your stuff." Rent the DVD of his old stand-up routine and think about it. It's just stuff. Happiness comes from connectedness to others. Money can't buy it, and stuff certainly can't create it. Create happiness with those around you. Start today. After you choose happiness, then choose abundance. Surround yourself with the things that express who you are, not things that define you.

MONEY IS NEITHER EVIL, DIRTY, NOR BAD.

MANY OF MY FRIENDS, PARTICULARLY FRIENDS OF MY CHILDREN, believe that abundance (in the financial sense) equates to selling your soul or abandoning your passions in life. Quite the opposite is true. You may have both. Money, in and of itself, is not the root of all evil, although the love/lust for money is. Focus on your passion, stay true to yourself, do what you love, and money will find you—no guilt required.

DON'T KEEP SCORE!

KEEPING SCORE, ESPECIALLY WITH A LOVED ONE, DOES NOT WORK. Once you are tracking every wrong done to you (using your rules, by the way), you will always give yourself credit and debit your loved one in a way beneficial to you. If you keep score, you are regarding yourself as better than the other person, which leads to resentment, revenge, and, in the case of a spouse, divorce.

RULE #1: DON'T FREAK OUT!

THIS HAS BEEN A RULE IN MY HOUSEHOLD FOR TWENTY YEARS, AND what a great rule it is, especially for kids, who are naturally prone to freaking out. Given a complex problem or emotional situation, when everyone is tense, when disaster is looming, when the sky is falling and terrorists are pounding at your door, freaking out will not make things better—so don't!

MORE BABIES WILL NOT FIX YOUR RELATIONSHIP OR YOUR BANK ACCOUNT (UNLESS YOU ARE AN OBSTETRICIAN).

MANY OF MY FRIENDS THINK THAT A BAD RELATIONSHIP MIGHT GET better if a baby (or another baby) is born. I can guarantee you that this is not the case. Children are not the glue that holds a relationship together. I know—everyone stays together in the bad times for the sake of the kids. But do you think you are doing your kids a favor by burdening them with the fact that their presence was responsible for the financial and emotional misery of their parents? Do everyone a favor and keep the innocent kids out of your screwed up relationship.

ALWAYS DOING WITHOUT AND SUFFERING IN SILENCE LEADS TO AN ANGRY, EMPTY LIFE.

SUFFERING AND PENNY-PINCHING MAY BE THE ONLY WAY OUT OF debt, but living on a shoestring budget when you don't have to will cause you to feel cheated when that truck runs you over at age forty-two. If you live in the future and never in the present, you will waste away. Find ways to enjoy the moments of now in life every day. Plan for the future, but live for today.

WHEN SOMEONE IS SACRIFICING, BLOOD IS BEING SHED.

SACRIFICE IS USUALLY SEEN AS A NOBLE THING. AFTER ALL, ACCORDING to Christian tradition, Jesus sacrificed his life for each of us. Isn't this the right and upstanding way to live? Well, you are not Jesus. You cannot save anyone else. Humans sacrifice each day for the sake of the perceived greater good. This is OK from time to time, if, for instance, we are talking about having Chinese for dinner when you really want Italian. Go ahead and sacrifice. But, if you cut off a limb to prove a point, you are the one who has to deal with the missing limb until the day you die.

SACRIFICE BEGETS RESENTMENT, WHICH BEGETS REVENGE.

THERE IS NO VARIABILITY IN THIS TRUTH. PAIN CAUSED BY ANOTHER for a long enough period of time will end poorly. Is it noble for a woman to sacrifice her dream of pursuing a business career for the sake of her husband and then for the sake of the kids and then she realizes that she is too old for more school? She will resent her husband, her kids, and herself forever (perhaps with a fake smile on her face).

REVENGE IS ALWAYS UGLY.

WHEN WAS THE LAST TIME YOU READ A *USA TODAY* STORY OF REVENGE that turned out well? The jealous wife runs over the cheating husband and they all live happily ever after? If you skim company profits to get back at your terrible boss, don't expect to get the satisfaction you seek, plus a raise and an extra week of paid time off. Pain is circular. Pain and revenge lead to more pain and revenge.

LEARN A SKILL THAT WOULD BE USEFUL IF YOU WERE ALONE IN THE WOODS.

I ONCE ASKED MYSELF SOMETHING VERY IMPORTANT: WHEN THE END of civilization as we know it comes, what good will I be at feeding myself or my family? What am I able to do with my own two hands? As a highly specialized physician, I need the support of technology, a top-notch hospital, and a good pharmacy. Without these things, I am pretty much worthless. If I at least knew which herb or plant root I could boil to heal a wound or relieve pain, I would have some useful skill. Take a course. Read a book. Have an ability that will help you survive in the event that you need it.

WHEN YOU GET INTO TROUBLE, SEEK HELP.

THE EGO IS THE BIGGEST OBSTACLE TO FINANCIAL FREEDOM. IT IS very difficult (especially for men) to ask for help, particularly about money. They often see it as an admission of failure or a blow to the root of their power. Many people would rather die than admit that they need help with money. Money means power. Money means love. Money means self-worth. But if you don't want to drown in your own financial disaster, swallow your ego and ask for help.

BEING LUCKY IS BETTER THAN BEING SMART!

LUCK KICKS BUTT EACH AND EVERY TIME. THE PROBLEM IS THAT luck is totally unpredictable. Relying on it is like relying on randomness. If you want luck, surround yourself by many people who seem lucky. Chances are that their good fortune is not luck at all, but skill that you didn't recognize previously.

AFTERWORD

PHYSICIANS, TRADITIONALLY, ARE THE WORST MONEY MANAGERS. Just as you shouldn't seek a plumber to help you grade a gemstone, you shouldn't ask a doctor for financial advice. What I have given to you in this book is not the advice of a doctor; it is the advice of time, experience, and years of study. I implore all of my readers to search their own souls for truth. If you read something that sounded valid, check it out, consider it, and act. Act now! Waiting for the "right time" will delay your actions into the "never" category.

It is my hope that each of my readers is impacted, even in the slightest way, to improve his or her personal, emotional, or financial life. Your comments are always welcome. Visit www.cha-chingwisdom.com.

ACKNOWLEDGMENTS

THIS WORK WAS INSPIRED BY ALL OF THE RELATIONSHIPS SO NEAR and dear to my life. To my parents, George and Marilyn Berry, for each modeling to me their unique gifts and support over four decades, "thank you" will never seem adequate. To Tiffany, Caitlyn, Amber, and Summer, you are each a source of daily strength and encouragement. To Toni, who showed me what it meant to think outside of the box. To Amy, for all of her amazing gifts and talents, who introduced to me the manifestation of true love and a real work ethic. To Malia, without whose drive and support this project would have sat on my computer for four more years. Finally, to all of my spiritual mentors who touched me through my life experiences and through books: Neale Donald Walsch, John McShane, Wayne Dyer, Deepak Chopra, Eckhart Tolle, Suze Orman, the late Joseph Campbell, and Wu Wei, the author of *I Ching Wisdom*.

ABOUT THE AUTHOR

DR. DAVID L. BERRY IS A SUCCESSFUL BUSINESSMAN, FATHER, INVENTOR, entrepreneur, amateur philosopher, physician, and specialist in complicated pregnancies. His unique life experience—he is a fourth-generation medical doctor on his mother's side and grew up with a PhD economist father—has given him an insightful way of thinking outside the box, both personally and professionally. He is the founder of Austin Perinatal Associates in Austin, Texas. He authored and implemented the business plan for the medical practice during his specialty training in maternal-fetal medicine. Dr. Berry currently lives in Austin and is the single father of four awesome girls.